Beyond Ecophobia

Reclaiming the Heart in Nature Education

DAVID SOBEL

Nature Literacy Series

Orion Readers are published by *Orion* magazine.

© 1996 The Orion Society
Second edition © 2013 The Orion Society

Orion
187 Main Street, Great Barrington, Massachusetts 01230
Telephone: 888/909-6568
Fax: 413/528-0676
www.orionmagazine.org

Design by Hans Teensma/Impress

Cover photograph by Molly Steinwald, www.mollysteinwald.com

ISBN: 978-1-935713-04-3

ORION'S NATURE LITERACY SERIES offers fresh educational ideas and strategies for cultivating "nature literacy"—the ability to learn from and respond to direct experience of nature. Nature literacy is not information gathered from a series of isolated, external "facts," but a deep understanding of natural and human communities. As such, it demands a far more integrated and intimate educational approach. Nature literacy means seeing nature as a connected, inclusive whole. Furthermore, it means redefining community as an interwoven web of nature and culture, a relationship marked by mutual dependence and one enriched and sustained by love. The materials presented in this series are directed to teachers, parents, and others concerned with creating an education that nurtures informed and active stewards of the natural world.

Other Books in the Nature Literacy Series:

Into the Field: A Guide to Locally Focused Learning, by Claire Walker Leslie, John Tallmadge, and Tom Wessels, with an introduction by Ann Zwinger.

Place-Based Education: Connecting Classrooms & Communities, by David Sobel.

CONTENTS

viii   **Introduction**
Jennifer Sahn

3   **Searching for a Cure**

9   **What's Important**

14   **Being in the Right Place at the Right Time: Honoring Stages of Development**

16   Empathy: Finding Animal Allies
Becoming Birds
Tiger, Tiger, Burning Bright
The Inner Amazon

23   Exploration: Teaching the Landscape
Watershed Wisdom
Stream Grooming
Following Streams

33   Social Action: Saving the Neighborhood
CAKE: Concern About Kids' Environment
The Forts
Bonding to the Self and Society

45 Taking Time: Allowing Communion
with Nature

48 References

50 Books for Children

INTRODUCTION

ALL ACROSS THE COUNTRY, from urban classrooms to one-room schoolhouses, children are learning about nature, using stories and games, computers and crayons, to gain an understanding of global warming, biodiversity, and how weather is made. The importance of transferring environmental values to the next generation is being recognized by preservationists and land-use planners alike. As a result of this increased appetite for nature education, teachers have been enthusiastically annexing all sorts of materials and lessons, without thinking specifically about what's appropriate and what's not. Now that environmental education has gone mainstream, it might behoove us to take a step back and consider the methods and messages of our teaching.

As adults we know the value of facts and figures, so we wish for children to know details about nature: names of trees and types of clouds and geologic formations. Yet the names won't stick unless there's a bedding of empathy where that knowledge can take root. And in our desire to prepare the next generation of adults to deal with the legacy of our ecological assaults, there is a tendency to inform children about the problems with the relationship between people and nature while failing to share with them its beautiful possibilities. In rushing to teach about global issues and the need for activism, we neglect the fact that young children have a fascination with the immediate, and an undying desire for sensory experience rather than conceptual generalization.

David Sobel's *Beyond Ecophobia: Reclaiming the Heart in Nature Education* presents environmental education strategies for teachers and parents of young people that cater to a child's natural affinities. By considering the developmental stages of childhood, Sobel suggests that there are appropriate environmental activities and accessible ecological concepts for children at different age levels that take into account their cognitive capabilities and psychological needs. The key is in allowing for a close relationship to develop between children and nature near home before laying the weight of the world's plight on their shoulders. Once children feel connected to the environment, physically and emotionally, they'll be compelled to seek the hard facts, and they'll take vested interest in healing the wounds of past generations while devising feasible, sustainable practices and policies for the future.

As parents, teachers, and members of our communities, we each can learn something from the observations in this thin volume. We not only find models for organic teaching and parenting here, but windows into our own childhood experiences, as well as our experiences with young people today. *Beyond Ecophobia* shows that the best teaching occurs when the emphasis is less on imparting knowledge and more on joining the child on a journey of discovery. If we can reimagine the world as a child sees it, while continuing to model attitudes of concern and respect for nature, our young companions will come to see the connections between loving the earth and caring for its well-being. En route, we might just learn something long forgotten since our own age of innocence.

JENNIFER SAHN
Editor, *Orion*

Beyond
Ecophobia

SEARCHING FOR A CURE

JUST AS ETHNOBOTANISTS are descending on tropical forests in search of new plants for medical uses, environmental educators, parents, and teachers are descending on second and third graders to teach them about the rainforests. From Brattleboro, Vermont, to Berkeley, California, school children are learning about tapirs, poison arrow frogs, and biodiversity. They hear the story of the murder of activist Chico Mendez and watch videos about the plight of indigenous forest people displaced by logging and exploration for oil. They learn that between the end of morning recess and the beginning of lunch, more than 10,000 acres of rainforest will be cut down, making way for fast food "hamburgerable" cattle.

The motive for all this is honorable and just: if children are aware of the problems of too many people utilizing too few resources, they will grow up to be adults who eat Rainforest Crunch, vote for environmental candidates, and buy energy efficient cars. They will learn that by recycling their *Weekly Readers* and milk cartons, at home and in school, they'll help save the planet. My fear is that just the opposite is occurring. In our zest for making them aware of and responsible for the world's problems, we cut our children off from their roots.

I confess to contributing money to the Children's Rainforest Project—a group that teaches kids about the rainforest and then funnels money raised from car washes and bake sales to the purchase of endangered lands in Costa Rica and Panama. At least this group doesn't just ring alarm bells; it gives kids a sense that they have the power to make things better. The currently popular term is "empowerment." But what really happens when we lay the weight of the world's environmental problems on eight- and nine-year-olds already haunted with too many concerns and not enough real contact with nature? Does the satisfaction of the check in the mail counterbalance the doom and the gloom? Janet Maslin, in a *New York Times* review of children's nature books, commented that: "It's not uncommon for even the most pleasant-looking children's books to have a similar scare factor, especially where the rain forest is concerned. . . . We do the children a disservice by shielding them unduly from a knowledge of the planet's problems. But we should think twice before making tots worry about toxins." Maslin continues:

> *The familiar old tales of ducks and bunnies may not have conveyed as many facts, but they were filled with whimsical possibilities that have no place in today's didactic children's literature. Bedtime stories of the past served the magical purpose of stirring children's imaginations, conjuring up a world of endless possibilities and then leaving young readers pleasantly sleepy. Today's versions, sounding the alarm over our shrinking hopes and resources, may leave them exhausted.*

If we fill our classrooms with examples of environmental abuse, we may be engendering a subtle form of dissociation. In response to physical and sexual abuse, children learn distancing techniques, ways to cut themselves off from the pain. In severe cases, children develop multiple personalities, other selves that aren't aware of the painful experiences. My fear is that our environmentally correct curriculum will end up distancing children from, rather than connecting them with, the natural world. The natural world is being abused and they just don't want to have to deal with it.

For *Childhood's Future*, a study of the changing nature of childhood at the end of the twentieth century, Richard Louv interviewed children, parents, community groups, and educators across the country. Visiting his own childhood neighborhood and elementary school, he talked with school children and noted that the relationship between children and nature has changed significantly in the last thirty years:

> *While children do seem to be spending less time physically in natural surroundings, they also seem to worry more about the disappearance of nature—in a global sense—than my generation did. . . . As a boy, I was intimate with the fields and the woods behind my house, and protective of them. Yet, unlike these children, I had no sense of any ecological degradation beyond my small natural universe.*

And in response to Louv's question of whether he liked to play indoors or outdoors better, one fourth grader proclaimed, "I like to play indoors better 'cause that's where the electrical outlets are." What's emerging is a strange kind of schizophrenia. Children are disconnected from the world outside their doors and connected with endangered animals and ecosystems around the globe through electronic media.

While children are studying the rainforest in school, they are not studying the northern hardwood forest, or even just the overgrown meadow outside the classroom door. Lucy Sprague Mitchell, a noted progressive educator and founder of Bank Street College of Education, spoke of the "here and now," the local forest and community, as a basis for her curriculum with six- through nine-year-olds. It is not until children are able to think logically and abstractly enough that she would embark on the "long ago and far away." Let us first cultivate an understanding of the habits and life cycles of chipmunks and milkweed—organisms children can study close at hand. By cultivating children's relationships with animals that lurk in the near recesses of their minds and forests, we can develop a taxonomy of relationships that will prepare them to gradually empathize with the animals of the rainforest. These are the foundation stones upon which an eventual understanding of ocelots and orchids can be built.

Some teachers have students learn about local forests and rainforests, and connect one to the other artfully, but many prefer rainforests because, from a curriculum perspective, they are much tidier to deal with. To study the northern hardwood forest, you have to send a note home to parents reminding them that the kids must wear boots next Tuesday. You have to deal with unruly kids, and wind blowing the clipboard paper all over the place. To study rainforests, you can stay inside and look at pretty pictures of all those strange and wonderful animals and make miniature cardboard rainforests safe within the confines of the classroom walls.

In the face of this dissociation, children still try to make ends meet, to connect the faraway and the close-by worlds. A mother recently shared an account of her eight-year-old daughter's afternoon project. Her daughter had been hard at work in the shed for more than an hour when she showed up in the kitchen with an elegant poster to be displayed at the general store across the street. Around an attractive illustration of a plump elephant read the bold edict, conceived in all seriousness: SAVE THE ELEPHANTS. DON'T USE IVORY SOAP. Saving endangered species is just as much a rage as saving the rainforest these days, and so a recent school project on African wildlife had motivated this girl to take protective action. The mistaken connection between the killing of elephants for their ivory tusks and the ingredients of Ivory Soap illustrates the child's desire to make the world right, to think globally and act locally. But wouldn't it be easier, and healthier, to both think and act locally at this age? Wouldn't it make more sense to have this child feel protective of the muskrats in the pond across the street?

The crux of the issue is the developmental appropriateness of environmental education curricula. In-depth rainforest curricula may be perfectly appropriate in middle or high school, but it doesn't belong in the primary grades. When I was training to be an elementary school teacher, my professor in a math methods course speculated that if we waited until sixth grade, we could teach all of elementary school mathematics in eight weeks. He didn't have the studies to back it up (How in the world would you find a group of parents willing to delay formal math instruction until children were eleven years old?), but his underlying message was intriguing. He believed that if we waited until children had the appropriate cognitive structures, and the appropriate experiential base in construction and cooking and crafts, then the abstractions of mathematics would be easy to teach.

One problem is premature abstraction. We teach too abstractly, too early. Mathematics instruction has been reinvigorated in the last two decades through the use of concrete materials (such as Cuisenaire rods, fraction bars, and Unifix cubes) and the grounding of math instruction in the stuff and problems of everyday life. The result has been the turning of the tide against math phobia. Mathematics educators realized that premature abstraction was one of the major causes of math phobia among children in the primary grades. Unable to connect the signs and symbols on the paper with the real world, many children were turning off to math. Adults describing their math phobia often date the beginning of their problems to third or fourth grade, when they just couldn't keep up any more. When math got hard, they tuned out, or perhaps from a psychological perspective, dissociated. They felt alienated from the world of numbers and computation and their math skills became frozen at the fourth-grade level. For adult math phobics, just the thought of multiplying fractions or long division makes them short of breath. As in any phobic reaction, the afflicted person feels unspecific anxiety and wants to flee from the situation. But with more child-centered math instruction, the problem of math phobia has diminished.

Perhaps to be replaced by ecophobia—a fear of ecological problems and the natural world. Fear of oil spills, rainforest destruction, whale hunting, acid rain, the ozone hole, and Lyme disease. Fear of just being outside. If we prematurely ask children to deal with problems beyond their understanding and control, prematurely recruit them to solve the mammoth problems of an adult world, then I think we cut them off from the possible sources of their strength. I propose that there are healthy ways to foster environmentally aware, empowered students. We can cure the malaise of ecophobia with ecophilia—supporting children's biological tendency to bond with the natural world.

WHAT'S IMPORTANT

A GRADUATE STUDENT of mine stumbled upon an intriguing discovery in his research with children last year. My assignment to the teachers-in-training was to conduct research that opened doors into the inner lives and thoughts of children. While some talked to children about the tooth fairy, animal classification, or the Pledge of Allegiance, Steve Moore wanted to find out what was *really* important to second graders. He selected twenty-five magazine pictures of children on bicycles, people playing baseball, happy families, toys, a dog, an eagle, pretty landscapes, farms, the Earth from space, workplaces, and the like. Then he encouraged children to choose three pictures that seemed important and talk about them.

Moore conducted his interviews with 40 seven and eight year olds in four different second grade classrooms in adjoining towns. When he analyzed his results, he found a curious pattern. The children's responses fell into two distinct groups, despite the fact that all four classrooms seemed quite similar on the surface. In two of the classrooms, children chose the picture of the earth from space, the eagle, and the deer. They talked about saving the planet, stopping pollution, and protecting eagles from extinction. They participated in the activity but didn't seem to really enjoy the process. In the other two classrooms, the children chose pictures of Legos, playing baseball, homes, and families as the important things in life. In the interviews, the children seemed energetic and enthusiastic to participate in the discussions.

When Moore saw this pattern, he returned to the classrooms, spoke to the teachers, and discovered a possible explanation for the differences. The first two classes had done an extensive Earth Week curriculum a couple of weeks before he conducted the interviews. Rainforest pictures were up on the walls, books and stories with environmental topics were in evidence, and one of these classes had just visited a new environmental education center. The second two classes had done very little in honor of Earth Week and had done almost no environmental curriculum recently. These teachers were a little sheepish about their apparent avoidance of these issues.

When he looked again at his results from this perspective, he found another pattern. In his total sample he found:

- 18 comments of *concern for the environment* (pollution, extinction, need for oxygen, etc.) All these comments were made by children in the Earth Week classes.

- 16 comments of *appreciation for the environment* (a place where we can live, I like birds, etc.) Seven of these comments were made by children in the Earth Week classes, nine were made by children in the non–Earth Week classes.

- 15 comments of *appreciation of families.* Fourteen of these were made by children in non–Earth Week classes and one by a child in an Earth Week class.

The result, from Moore's perspective, was a kind of de-spondency among the children in the Earth Week classroom and a submerging of children's natural interests in a sea of problems. He reports:

> *The whole issue of the Earth Week curriculum was a big eye opener to me. The interview patterns suggest that kids who had spent a week or more working on environmental issues were fully taken in by them. The Earth Week group made choices that were heavily weighted with concerns about the Earth, the animals, homeless children. The non–Earth Week classes made choices about playing, about families, about having fun. It is my impression that the Earth Week work pretty much blew the doors off these kids' fun interests. I think we need to be careful about this kind of curricular brainwashing with children of this age.*

Though clearly not an exhaustive study, Moore's findings resonate eerily with a study conducted in West Germany during the 1980's. Concerned about acid rain effects on German forests, the ozone hole, heavy-metal pollution in European rivers, the aftermath of Chernobyl, and other environmental problems, the Germans implemented a conscientious national curriculum endeavor. The intent was to raise the consciousness of the elementary student body throughout the country regarding environmental problems. By informing students about the problems and showing them how they could participate in finding the solutions, the education ministry hoped to create empowered global citizens. Follow-up studies conducted some years after implementation indicated just the opposite had occurred. As a result of the curriculum initiative, education officials found that students felt hopeless and disempowered. The problems were seemingly so widespread and beyond their control that the students tended to turn away from, rather than face up to, participating in local attempts at problem solving.

If curriculum focused on saving the earth doesn't work, what does? One way to find the answer is to figure out what contributes to the development of environmental values in adults. What happened in the childhoods of environmentalists, some researchers have asked, to make them grow up with strong ecological values? A handful of studies like this have been conducted, and when Louise Chawla of Kentucky State University reviewed them for her article "Children's Concern for the Natural Environment" in *Children's Environments Quarterly*, she found a striking pattern. Most environmentalists attributed their commitment to a combination of two sources: "many hours spent outdoors in a keenly remembered wild or semi-wild place in childhood or adolescence, and an adult who taught respect for nature." Not one of the conservationists surveyed explained his or her dedication as a reaction against exposure to an ugly environment.

What a simple solution. No rainforest curriculum, no environmental action, just opportunities to be in the natural world with modeling by a responsible adult.

When the Sierra Club wants to raise money for saving old-growth forests, they send photographs of denuded, eroding hillsides with their donation requests. Defenders of Wildlife raises money by showing us the cuddly harp seal with big black eyes being bludgeoned to death. For adults with a commitment to preservation and a sense of self firmly in place, this technique appropriately motivates us to action. For young children, children in kindergarten through third or fourth grade, this technique is counterproductive.

Lurking underneath "environmentally correct" curricula is

the assumption that if children see the horrible things that are happening, then they too will be motivated to make a difference. But those images can have an insidious, nightmarish effect on young children whose sense of time, place, and self are still forming. Newspaper pictures of homes destroyed by California wildfires are disturbing to my seven-year-old New Hampshire daughter because she immediately personalizes them. "Is that fire near here? Will our house burn down? What if we have a forest fire?" she queries, because for her, California is right around a psychic corner.

What's important is that children have an opportunity to bond with the natural world, to learn to love it and feel comfortable in it, before being asked to heal its wounds. John Burroughs remarked that "Knowledge without love will not stick. But if love comes first, knowledge is sure to follow." Our problem is that we are trying to invoke knowledge, and responsibility, before we have allowed a loving relationship to flourish.

BEING IN THE RIGHT PLACE AT THE RIGHT TIME: HONORING STAGES DEVELOPMENT

WE OFTEN REFER to moments of wondrous happenstance as being in the right place at the right time. Curriculum often isn't and it's usually too early. To get a sense of when to study rainforests or endangered species, to understand how to practice developmentally appropriate environmental education, we need a scheme, a big picture, of the relationship between the natural world and the development of the person.

The formative years of bonding with the earth include three stages of development that should be of primary concern to parents and teachers: early childhood from ages four to seven, the elementary years from eight to eleven, and early adolescence from twelve to fifteen. Though these age frames need to be considered flexibly, my belief is that environmental education should have a different tenor and style during each of these stages.

Over the past ten years, I have collected neighborhood maps from hundreds of children in the United States, England,

and the Caribbean. Through analyzing these maps and doing interviews and field trips with these same children, I have
found clear patterns of development in the relationship between the child and his or her expanding natural world.

From age four until about seven, children's homes fill the
center of their maps and much of their play is within sight or
earshot of the home. The house and yard are the significant
world for them. Children often describe the worms, chipmunks, and pigeons that live in their yards or on their blocks
and feel protective about these creatures.

From eight to eleven, children's geographical ranges expand rapidly. Their maps push off the edge of the page and
they often need to attach extra pieces of paper to map the new
terrain they are investigating. Children's homes become small,
inconsequential, and often move to the periphery of the map.
The central focus in their maps is the "explorable landscape."

From twelve to fifteen, the maps continue to expand in
scope and become more abstract, but the favored places often
move out of the woods and into town. Social gathering places
such as the mall, the downtown luncheonette, and the town
park take on new significance.

At each of these stages, children desire immersion, solitude, and interaction in a close, knowable world. We take
children away from these strength-giving landscapes when we
ask them to deal with distant ecosystems and environmental
problems. Rather, we should be attempting to engage children
more deeply in knowing the flora, fauna, and character of their
own local places. The woods behind the school and the neighborhood streets and stores are the places to start.

How do we translate these notions into guidelines for environmental education? I propose three phases of environmental
curricula during the elementary and middle school years. In
early childhood, activities should center on enhancing the de-

velopmental tendency toward empathy with the natural world; in middle childhood, exploration should take precedence; and in early adolescence, social action should assume a more central role. The character and style of each of these stages is illustrated in the following sections through stories of developmentally appropriate teaching and parenting.

EMPATHY: FINDING ANIMAL ALLIES

Empathy between the child and the natural world should be a main objective for children ages four through seven. As children begin their forays out into the natural world, we can encourage feelings for the creatures living there. Early childhood is characterized by a lack of differentiation between the self and the other. Children feel implicitly drawn to baby animals; a child feels pain when someone else scrapes her knee. Rather than force separateness, we want to cultivate that sense of connectedness so that it can become the emotional foundation for the more abstract ecological concept that everything is connected to everything else. Stories, songs, moving like animals, celebrating seasons, and fostering Rachel Carson's "sense of wonder" should be primary activities during this stage.

Cultivating relationships with animals, both real and imagined, is one of the best ways to foster empathy during early childhood. Children want to run like deer, to slither along the ground like snakes, to be clever as a fox and quick like a bunny. There's no need for endangered species here—there are more than enough common, everyday species to fill the lives of children. And the environmentally correct notion of not anthropomorphizing animals can be thrown out the window. Paul Shepard, in *The Arc of the Mind*, says:

*Animals have a magnetic affinity for the child, for
each in its way seems to embody some impulse, reaction, or movement that is 'like me.' In the playful,
controlled enactment of them comes a gradual mastery
of the personal inner zoology of fears, joys and relationships. In stories told, their forms spring to life in
the mind, re-presented in consciousness, training the
capacity to imagine.*

With this conviction in mind, a group of colleagues and I
conducted the following activities with preschool children at
the Happy Valley School in Peterborough, New Hampshire,
and with first and second graders at Camp Waubenong in
Brattleboro, Vermont.

Becoming Birds

I have always been resistant to bird curricula with children.
Part of this stems from my own childhood sense that watching and naming birds was dumb. Somehow, it never appealed
to me until I was in my early twenties. I worry when ardent
bird watchers and environmentalists try to foist their enthu-
siasms on unsuspecting five-, six-, and seven-year-olds. On
the other hand, birds are fascinating and beautiful creatures,
and many children are entranced by them. (A personal note:
When my wife suggested, four years ago, that we get a cockatiel for our five-year-old daughter, Tara, my hackles went up.
"What? Buy a bird plundered from the rainforest by bounty
hunters!?" When she assured me that these cockatiels were
born and bred in Massachusetts, I consented, albeit unenthu-
siastically. The relationship that has developed between my
daughter, Tara, and Lily, the cockatiel, has been a joy to watch.
The emotional connection between them is moving and Lily

has inspired countless hours of movement exploration, poring over picture books, drawing pictures, and writing about birds.)

We initiated our bird curriculum planning at Camp Waubenong by agreeing that we wouldn't have the children identify birds from fleeting glimpses and then look them up in books to start. Boring! Rather, we speculated on what it is about birds that appeals to children. The answer was obvious: they fly and they make nests. Applying the developmental principle that children like to *become* things rather than objectify them in early childhood, we came up with our plan.

We gathered a bunch of large refrigerator boxes, cut them into sheets, and had the children lie down on top of them, on their backs with their arms outstretched. Starting at the neck, we traced around the children, but instead of following along the underside of the arm, we drew a straight line from their wrists to their waists then down on both sides to about the knees. The children then stood up, we cut out the shape, and voila!, each child had an individualized set of wings. We strapped them on, made it clear that the children were not to try the wings out by jumping off roofs, and they were off. A flock of birds leaped into action, flying through the forest, exploring life as birds. We made it to the meadow where hay had been recently cut and said, if we're birds, we need nests. And so we made child-sized nests. Many hours of dramatic play followed.

A few days later we said, "We've been thinking. You all make great birds, but we noticed that you're all brown and the birds we see around here, well some of them are brown, but some of them have lots of colors. What are some of the color patterns on birds?" Children described some birds they had seen, but we didn't make a point of teaching names. Instead, we pulled out the paints so they could paint their wings. More bird games followed. By the next day, children started to notice the birds around camp. "Hey, that's the same bird as me, that's the color pattern on my wings." Then the bird *books* came out. Soon we had children poring over bird books trying to identify what kinds of birds they were and learn what they ate. Because we had started at their level of developmental fascination, had facilitated empathy through their participation in bird consciousness, we prepared them to objectify and enter the more cognitive realm of bird knowledge.

Tiger, Tiger, Burning Bright

A few summers ago, my six-year-old daughter participated in a week-long program led by a dancer and an environmental educator. The task for the week was to create a dance/ritual performance based on the children's relationship with animals. To find those connections, Diana Reno, the educator, led children on short, guided-imagery forays to find an animal friend. Adapting the technique of shamanic journeying, Reno had children find a comfortable place in the forest and close their eyes. As she drummed, the children waited to see who would come to visit them. Each night, when we asked Tara about her day, she enthusiastically described her animal encounters, always in a tone of voice that indicated that these weren't just imaginings, but real events:

> *I met my animal friend and she was a Tiger and I was a baby tiger. We went to go hunting and we saw a baby elephant and I jumped on it's back and tried to bite it. But the baby elephant screeched in my ear (and here she gets a grimace on her face showing the pain of the loudness) and I fell off the elephant's back. We went on and we found a rabbit and I grabbed it with my teeth and shook it till it died. We brought it back to the Tiger's*

cave. I turned back into me so I could start a fire and cook it on a stick and then I turned back into a baby tiger so we could eat it and it was delicious.

I was amazed at both the vividness of her accounts and at her enthusiastic carnivorousness. This is not what I expected from my gentle, sometimes squeamish daughter. Tara's most significant stuffed animal since she was one year old—the one we live in fear of losing—is a rabbit named Bun-Bun. When Tara is upset and in need of solace, she runs to find Bun-Bun. (If any stuffed animal was ever to become real, like the Velveteen Rabbit, Bun-Bun would certainly be a candidate.) Tara has a long relationship with fairies, is dedicated to saving and taking care of small animals, and has flirted with vegetarianism. I was surprised that it was a tiger who came as her animal friend.

After much reflection, I speculated that the tiger may be symbolic of Tara's developmental shift from early to middle childhood, from empathy to exploration. Perhaps the tiger eating the rabbit is indicative of her move out of early childhood, symbolized by the rabbit, and into middle childhood, symbolized by the powerful and self-sufficient tiger. Here was Tara eating her transitional object, internalizing an aspect of her younger self, and embracing a new, stronger, more independent aspect of her self.

Since this experience, we have started to talk to Tara about her tiger self. When she is timid, or fearful, or feels overpowered by other children or events, we encourage her to become her tiger self, to feel her strength and power. By using her sense of tigerness, we can invite her to find that aspect of herself that is like a tiger. This is the "personal inner zoology" to which Paul Shepard was referring. Drawing on children's empathic relationship with animals, Tara's teachers structured activities that provided a path for self-development. For children in early and middle childhood, this seems like appropriate, potent environmental education.

The Inner Amazon

The development of a personal inner zoology continues to be an appropriate objective in environmental education through adolescence and into adulthood. Joanna Macy and John Seed's Council of All Beings work invites adults to identify and empathize with animals as a way of becoming more whole, and more committed to environmental action. While our tendency with older children is to be historical, logical, and socially active, it is important to continue cultivating empathic relationships with animals during adolescence.

Brenda Peterson, writing in the Spring 1993 issue of *Orion* magazine, describes her environmental work through storytelling with inner-city adolescents in Seattle. After just a few days of a two-week program, one girl shares a story of her best friend being murdered in a drive-by shooting, and the whole tenor of the class changes. Peterson calls the students together and says:

> We're going to talk story the way they used to long ago
> when people sat around at night in circles just like this
> one. That was a time when we still listened to animals
> and trees and didn't think ourselves so alone in this world.
> Now we're going to carry out jungle justice and find
> Katie's killer. We'll call him before our tribe. All right?
> Who wants to begin our story?

What follows is a remarkable account of group storytelling in which each child becomes a jungle animal and plays a part in tracking down the murderer. Complete with masks and movement, the children enact the drama that they tell. Peterson reflects:

> *Many of these teenagers have barely been in the woods; in fact, many inner city kids are afraid of nature. . . . These kids are not environmentalists who worry about saving nature. And yet, when imagining an Amazon forest too thick for weapons to penetrate, too primitive for their futuristic Pac-Man battles, they return instinctively to their animal selves. These are animals they have only seen in zoos or on television, yet there is a profound identification, an ease of inhabiting another species that portends great hope for our own species's survival. Not because nature is "out there" to be saved or sanctioned, but because nature is in them. The ancient, green world has never left us though we have long ago left the forest.*
>
> *What happens when we call upon our inner landscape to connect with the living rainforests still left in the natural world? I believe our imagination can be as mutually nurturing as an umbilical cord between our bodies and the planet. As we told our Amazon stories over the next week of class . . . we could feel the rainforest growing in that sterile classroom. Lights low, surrounded by serpents, the jaguar clan, the elephants, I'd as often hear growls, hisses, and howls as words. Between this little classroom and the vast Amazon rainforest stretched a fine thread of story that grew thicker each day, capable of carrying our jungle meditations.*

It's striking to me that these children entered the rainforests of their imaginations not to save endangered species, but to save one child from grief and despair. Even for adolescents sophisticated enough to begin to grasp the profoundness of the rainforest problem, the doorway was dealing with a personal problem that confronted one of their group. Peterson reminds us that "by telling their own animal stories [children] are practicing ecology at its most profound and healing level. Story as ecology—it's so simple, something we've forgotten. In our environmental wars, the emphasis has been on saving species, not *becoming* them." And so we must begin in empathy, by becoming the animals before we can save them.

EXPLORATION: TEACHING THE LANDSCAPE

Exploring the nearby world and knowing your place should be a primary objective for the bonding with the earth stage, from ages seven to eleven. The curriculum can mirror the expanding scope of the child's significant world, focusing first on the surroundings of the home and school, then the neighborhood, the community, the region, and beyond. Making forts, creating small imaginary worlds, hunting and gathering, searching for treasures, following streams and pathways, exploring the landscape, taking care of animals, gardening and shaping the earth can be primary activities during this stage. Jean Craighead George's books such as *My Side of the Mountain* and *Julie of the Wolves* capture the thrill of living completely off the land that captivates children toward the end of this stage.

The desire to explore the landscape becomes a potent force during these years and many prominent writers and naturalists claim that their feelings of connection with the natural world emerged during this life phase. In his book

The Lord's Woods, the prominent ornithologist Robert Arbib captures well this exploratory drive, recalling:

> *I was nine years old that June afternoon so many years ago when we first discovered the Lord's Woods and the world was unspoiled and filled with mysteries. My first two-wheeler, dark red and fast, had come with my birthday in March, and ever since that glorious day my world had been expanding. Only yesterday I had ventured beyond the edge of my universe, out where Westwood Road ceased to be paved and wound into the endless green unknown of the forest. . . .*
>
> *We will know it all, Carl and I. We will explore and conquer this America of ours, we will make this our private paradise. To know it and, by knowing, own it, and then go forth beyond our woodland bounds, answering the urgent beckonings of field and farm and road and stream, the distant marsh horizon . . . and the row of trees beyond the last ones we can see.*

Annie Dillard, in *An American Childhood,* recalls the urban equivalent of this experience growing up in Pittsburgh around the age of ten:

> *I pushed at my map's edges. Alone at night I added newly memorized streets and blocks to old streets and blocks, and imagined connecting them on foot. . . . On darkening evenings I came home exultant, secretive, often from some exotic leafy curb a mile beyond what I had known at lunch, where I had peered up at the street sign, hugging the cold pole, and fixed the intersection in my mind. What joy, what relief, eased me as I pushed*

*open the heavy front door!—joy and relief because, from
the trackless waste, I had located home, family and the
dinner table once again.*

At the same time as the child's home becomes less significant and the landscape looms large, forts and dens show up
on children's maps. These special places of childhood, both
found and built places, appear to be crucially important for
many children from ages eight to eleven. Children in urban,
suburban, and rural landscapes find and create hidden places,
even in daunting circumstances. Kim Stafford describes his
special place in park land on the edge of Portland, Oregon, in
his essay "The Separate Hearth":

> *Here was my private version of civilization, my separate
> hearth. Back Home, there were other versions of this. I
> would take any refuge from the thoroughfare of plain liv-
> ing—the doll-house, the tree-house, furniture, the table-
> cloth tent, the attic, the bower in the cedar tree. I would
> take any platform or den that got me above, under, or
> around the corner from the everyday. There I pledged
> allegiance to what I knew, as opposed to what was com-
> mon. My parents' house was a privacy from the street,
> from the nation, from the rain. But, I did not make that
> house, or find it, or earn it with my own money. It was
> given to me. My separate hearth had to be invented by
> me, kindled, sustained, and held secret by my own soul
> as a rehearsal for departure.*

And Richard Louv quotes a fifth grader describing her
home in the woods: "When I'm in the woods, I feel like I'm
in my mother's shoes . . . it feels like that's where I should
go, like it's your home, and you can do anything you want to

because there's not anyone bothering you. You have the woods to yourself."

These new homes in the wild, and the journeys of discovering them, are the basis for bonding with the natural world. We need to cultivate a sensitivity to this developmental geography of childhood. Appropriate curriculum at this age will capitalize on the child's innate drive to explore the nearby world.

Watershed Wisdom

The Brookwood School in Manchester, Massachusetts, has recently revised its science curriculum to focus on aquatic environments, taking advantage of the range of watery places accessible from the school. Starting with woodland streams in first grade, the curriculum moves down the watershed to ponds in second grade, freshwater wetlands in third grade, and eventually out to the ocean by eighth grade. The first graders' streams are right outside the science classroom's door, the ponds are a bit of a walk, and the ocean is a half mile away, so the curriculum expands outward along with the scope of the children's interests and cognitive capabilities.

Structuring the curriculum like a watershed makes organic sense and calls into question the way in which we routinely teach the water cycle. The teaching of the water cycle has always been one of my pet peeves. Starting in first grade, children do little experiments in jars and soon thereafter draw diagrams of clouds, condensation, rivers flowing to the ocean and evaporating back to the clouds. Too often the denatured words have little connection to the real world. Rarely do children step outside, investigate puddles, collect rainwater, make miniature landscapes, or follow streams. Instead, they draw the same diagram, ad nauseam, throughout the elementary years.

I remember working with a group of fourth, fifth, and sixth graders who could all recite the water cycle forwards and backwards. To test the depth of their understanding, I asked, "When it rains over the ocean, does it rain fresh water or salt water?" Almost all of them were adamant that it rained salt water. If we were teaching the water cycle in an experiential fashion, these children would know the answer to this question. But the problem is that we're not really teaching science or environmental education, we are teaching a veneer of words, recitation without reality.

The water cycle isn't something to be taught in two weeks; it's best done over the six or eight years of elementary and middle school. The water courses of the landscape are the circulatory system of the living earth, and we can only learn them by following them, literally and metaphorically. The concepts and content of the water cycle are teachable and accessible, but only with a raft of tangible, concrete experiences to carry us through the process.

Stream Grooming

Four springs ago, I initiated a Tuesday morning activity of stream play and stream grooming with my own children. We focused on a little stream that crosses a wood lot we own a few miles from our house. As I was home with the children on Tuesdays, the possibility of doing this again and again throughout the spring appealed to me.

The idea was to choose a section of the stream and clean it out: remove sticks and leaf debris, make the waterfalls prettier, create an openness in the woods next to the stream. Of course I did most of the work while they messed about. They tested the thickness of remnant ice, made leaf boats, tried to find deep spots, dissected rotten logs, hopped across from one side to the other, got their feet wet. Then, after about an hour, we'd sit down for a snack and a story.

One day, after lots of cleaning, I told a story about two children and their father who go to clean out a stream. I repeated the exact sequence of events of that morning, up to the point where the father is telling a story, and then new things start to happen. In the story, a bird comes flitting through the woods and they hear her as she flies down and notices all the nice little bathtubs that have been created. The children watch as she bathes herself and flies away. Then a rabbit comes, is pleased at how much cleaner the water looks, and takes a long, cool drink. Finally, a squirrel visits, notices there's a nice patch of open ground next to the stream, and happily starts to look for acorns. At that point, we actually looked through the duff on the forest floor and found acorns, as does the squirrel in the story.

Without being too heavy handed, my hope was to create firsthand experiences with how streams work, where they go, and how they behave, and to posit the notions of caretaking and stewardship, but at a very close and personal level. From this experience, we graduated to walking the narrow, cliff-clinging trail along the stream through Eliza Adams Gorge behind our house in New Hampshire. And then to an ongoing search for waterfall swimming holes along Quebrada Honda not far from our current home-away-from-home in the mountains of Costa Rica. The children are as playful in these streams as otters, sliding and splashing with glee, and we always clean the stream as we go. Walking back from a recent outing, Tara and Eli slipped into their ongoing fantasy game when Tara said, "Now, let's pretend that we live alone in the forest and this stream is our home." This is exactly the emotional connection I want my children to have with the watersheds they live in.

Following Streams

For elementary school children, appropriate environmental education about the water cycle can start by engaging children with running water. Many children who can recite the water cycle verbally still draw maps that have streams running uphill. The challenge for the teacher is to find ways to engage students in stream walking and stream studies. Both of the following examples teach the water cycle in concrete, tangible, and exciting ways—ways that extend childrens' authentic interests in streams.

In Judy Fink's third grade classroom in Keene, New Hampshire one spring, the water cycle curriculum included all the traditional diagrams and recitations, but it went far beyond that. The curriculum was based on the wonderful book *Paddle-to-the-Sea*, by Holling C. Holling, a story about a boy who carves a canoe and an Indian out of wood and lets them go in the upper reaches of the Great Lakes. The story, in beautiful narrative and illustrations, chronicles the adventures and mishaps of this carved boat as it makes its way down to the St. Lawrence and out to sea. Most teachers would stop after reading the book. But in this classroom, the teacher had each child create his or her own boat. There was discussion about form and function, longevity, and of what kind of messages they might include on their boats. Then the children walked from the school to the Old Stone Arch Bridge over the Ashuelot River, a tributary of the Connecticut. With a simple ritual celebration, they launched all the boats, hoping that the people who found them would phone and account for how far they had traveled.

Three weeks later, one of the students received this letter in the mail:

Dear Brendan,

On the 18th of this month, I was canoeing on the Ashuelot River. I put in up by the Surry Mountain Dam and paddled down to the waterfall by Taco Bell. I found your boat about 500 yards up from the water-fall, caught in some weeds and bushes. I took it home and was going to call you to see if you wanted me to re-release it. I have decided the message was clear enough. "PUT ME BACK IN THE WATER." So that's what I will do today.

The boat is still in pretty good shape. . . . Good luck with the rest of your trip. I hope you get more correspondence and the boat makes it to the ocean. If you would like to write me a letter, I would be curious to know where you put it in the water, when you put it in, and how far it went.

Your fellow river runner,
Harold S. Pike III

The experience of receiving the letter served to authenti-cate the activity for all the students in the class. Yes, the river actually carried their boats part of the way to the sea, and this one, at least, was still on its way. The teacher and students found the location where the boat was discovered on the map and speculated about where it might be now. The letter also let the students know that there were other people out there exploring rivers and streams. Tying the children in with the real world, this activity demonstrated to them that the way in which water flows through the environment is an interesting and important thing to know.

David Millstone, a fifth grade teacher in Norwich, Vermont, had similar objectives when he organized a stream-following expedition with his class. Recognizing the allure of stream following and the potential curricular value, he decided to try something unusual. He initiated a class expedition to follow a stream, not knowing where the stream would lead them. In a student-produced newspaper about this expedition, one child wrote:

The Deep Dark Dungeon

"I can't see five feet," I thought to myself. We were walking through a giant culvert following this stream that runs behind the school and through the Nature Area.

"Watch out, dripping water," Mr. Millstone warned us. I finally realized what is beyond the steel grates that you see along the street. I looked up it and saw the grate twenty feet above me. The culvert seemed to be moving. I think we took a turn somewhere.

"The end," someone shouted.... I had to walk with my feet widely apart. We got out alive, had a snack and continued on our adventure."

Millstone, in an introduction to the newsletter, describes his motives:

We went for the Great Hike Downstream for many rea-

sons. I was curious about the stream myself, and found in conversations with others that no one really seemed to know where the stream went. The trip expanded our recent emphasis on mapping Norwich neighborhoods. The search would challenge the class's map-making skills; similarly, an adventure into the unknown would stimulate children's writing. . . . The experience of following a stream would reinforce a fundamental concept in topographic maps—water flows downhill. The stream flows directly under the new playground, the area which we will be surveying for our own contour map. I wanted children to experience the thrill of posing a question and working directly to find the answer. And not least of all, I thought this trip would be fun.

Like any true adventure, what started out as a simple idea grew more complex as we trudged along. We ended up doing things that I had not anticipated, and going where I had not planned to go. There was valuable learning for both children and adults in dealing with the unexpected.

The children's writing for the class newsletter crackles with excitement over discovering something literally in their backyard. And notice that neither of these projects touches directly on acid rain or groundwater pollution or drinking-water quality or evaporation and condensation. They both, however, immerse children in the primary experience of exploring streams and understanding, in a personal way, where they go. Wet sneakers and muddy clothes are prerequisites for understanding the water cycle.

SOCIAL ACTION: SAVING THE NEIGHBORHOOD

Social action appropriately begins around age twelve and certainly extends beyond age fifteen. While woods, parks, and playgrounds are the landscapes of middle childhood, adolescents want to be downtown. As children start to discover the "self" of adolescence and feel their connectedness to society, they naturally incline toward wanting to save the world. Managing school recycling programs, passing town ordinances, testifying at hearings, planning and going on school expeditions are all appropriate activities at this point. Though often used with younger children, Lynne Cherry's *A River Runs Wild*, about the restoration of the Nashua River initiated by one committed person, serves as an excellent model for how students can contribute to their communities. Developmentally sensitive school programs will also recognize the need for rites of passage toward the end of this period. Initiation signifies the transition into adulthood with the dual challenges of solitude and social responsibility.

My policy with social action activities is: NO TRAGEDIES BEFORE FOURTH GRADE. First, let me define tragedies. Tragedies are big, complex problems beyond the geographical and conceptual scope of young children. Rainforest destruction is an environmental tragedy. The Valdez oil spill and the genocide of Muslims in the Bosnian war are tragedies. As subjects for curriculum, these topics should not be considered prior to fourth grade, and in most cases, well beyond that. The defining question should be: *When do children have the emotional and cognitive readiness for dealing with overwhelmingly sad and conceptually complex issues?*

Dealing with the nearby sadnesses of events in children's

lives is a different matter. Parents getting divorced, pets dying, a favorite tree being cut down are necessary and appropriate tragic issues to deal with in the early elementary grades. But children deserve to be spared the plight of endangered species and the destruction of old-growth forests until they have the emotional fortitude and ego strength to deal with the vastness of our ecological plight.

In reference to a developmental study of children's ecological attitudes in the *Journal of Environmental Education* by Stephen Kellert, Louise Chawla and Roger Hart comment:

> *That ethical concerns and ecological appreciation increase after age twelve conforms to the stage of formal operations, in which adolescents begin to conceive of an abstract universe of relations. [We believe] that ecological thinking is especially dependent upon the attainment of abstract thinking because most ecological cycles are too extended in time and space or too microscopic to be directly perceived.*

Asking young students to study ecological problems before they have developed the power of abstract thinking invites them to draw oversimplified conclusions. In his paper about second graders, Steve Moore cautions:

> *[When teachers] present the destruction of the rainforest in the primary years, I rarely see or hear consideration of the many sides of this complex issue. We see people involved in environmental destruction, but for them it's a matter of having enough food and land to survive. For loggers in the Pacific Northwest, the spotted owl does threaten the way they've lived for a long time. We don't like what they're doing, but meanwhile they may have a*

*difficult time paying their mortgages and educating their
children if logging is halted. Were any of us in their shoes,
we might find it difficult to be rational and opt for job
retraining, relocation and a lost lifestyle just to keep our
heads above water and save some owls' breeding territory.*

This kind of balanced understanding is somewhat beyond
the ken of normal third graders, so instead we settle for easy
dichotomies. Ocelots are good and bulldozer drivers are bad.
This doesn't mean that we should stonewall children when
they inquire about rainforests. Rather, we can answer their
questions reassuringly and make our curriculum decisions
based on accessible content and realizable goals.

When my son comes home and says, "They're burning
down a football field of rainforest every minute and we have
to save it!" I respond with two connected strategies. First I
say, "Yes, some rainforests are being burned down and there
are a lot of people working to save them. Some people are
even helping grow new rainforests where old ones have been
burned down." I acknowledge the truth and reassure him that
responsible adults are working on the problem. Then I say,
"You know there are things we can do to make our forests
healthier here in New Hampshire and you can help," and I try
to enlist his help in managing our wood lot for cordwood and
wildlife habitat or in pruning the apple trees. Similarly, curriculum that focuses on environmental problems will be most
successful when it starts in fifth or sixth grade and focuses on
local problems where children can make a real difference.

CAKE: Concerns About Kids' Environment

In an article by Paul Karr in the April 1990 issue of Sanctuary,
Bridget Sullivan's mother recalls that Bridget and her class-

mates decided to start CAKE when they learned about global warming. The children had been bombarded by graphic images of dying fish, scarred trees, rising sea level—the kinds of images children usually associate with nuclear war. "She was afraid that she would have to live underground. . . . She was afraid the world would get so hot it would explode, afraid her children could not experience the joy of nature." Encouraged by teachers and parents to do something to confront their fears, a group of eight- to eleven-year-olds started an after-school group to protect their environment.

The children conducted a survey of the roadside waste in their home town of Freeport, Maine, and found that half of the trash was styrofoam. The children had learned that the production of styrofoam releases CFCs into the atmosphere, which eat away at ozone and contribute to global warming. Thus they decided to petition the town council to ban the use of styrofoam containers in the town. This put them head to head with the local McDonald's, the source of much of the styrofoam. A lengthy legal battle with high-priced out-of-town lawyers was decided in the kids' favor and the local McDonald's was one of the first in the world to eliminate its trademark foam containers.

After their initial success, CAKE members went on to testify in support of strict auto-emission standards in the state capitol, clean up a local park, and, yes, help in getting classes on rainforest ecology in the local school. This successful campaign has had national coverage on "The Today Show" and in *World* magazine, and many of the CAKE members speak to other children's groups interested in environmental activism.

The Forts

One of the most intriguing aspects of the CAKE story, however, never made it into the news. Most of the children in CAKE came from the George Soule School in South Freeport, a progressive, alternative public school. One of the long-standing traditions at the Soule School was the Forts, a children's cultural inheritance since the school was built about twenty-five years ago. The Forts area comprises about three quarters of an acre of wooded space with a little underbrush adjacent to the school playground. Here groups of children build structures from old tree limbs and other scavenged natural material. Over the years, an autonomous children's culture has been allowed to evolve, almost completely independent of adult or teacher intervention. The Forts is a children's world and children are encouraged to work out problems there independently. When the Forts were studied by Patrice Maynard during the spring of 1990, she described that:

> *Teachers would become a bit annoyed when asked to*
> *mediate arguments about Forts. It was made clear that*
> *Forts were kid things, and arguments should be kept and*
> *settled there. Teachers made it clear that they would only*
> *intervene if they absolutely had to, and then if they did*
> *have to, they made it clear through their demeanor that*
> *it was not what they wanted to be doing.*

In the spring of 1990, about 40 second through fifth graders were actively involved in sustaining six to seven forts. Some forts were elaborate. The fifth graders' fort included a castle, a bank, a gate of entry, and covered the largest area. Of striking interest was the monetary system that emerged based on chunks of blacktop that had been broken up. This blacktop, with high mica content, glittered more than average blacktop. With surprising consistency, children agreed about the relative worth of different sized chunks. Maynard describes that

a four inch wide chunk of the stuff universally elicited a
$20 valuation from a dozen children. This money can
be traded for different commodities. Corn, for instance is
a necessity. Corn is a food and if one's fort has no corn,
it is without food. Corn is actually dried cinnamon fern
and a bunch of corn about an inch in diameter at the
stems costs $20.

This consistency, as well as the clearly agreed-upon fort
rules, testify to the elaboration of child-owned traditions that
have stabilized over the years. In reflecting on the significance
of the Forts in helping to shape the children's environmental
ethics, Maynard comments:

The depth of the personal feelings woven into the rules
and unspoken proprieties of Fort activities is impres-
sive. It is this that leads to the speculation that the very
existence of the Forts allows for a level of consciousness
about the environment, about the earth, not possible
without them. Violations of the Fort area are equivalent
to personal violations.

One weekend, there were marauders who vandalized the
whole Fort area and took some things out of the Forts
and uncovered secret places. It took several days of small
meetings that were like therapy sessions to settle every-
one's feelings about the incident. The children took it
very personally. It would seem that this is an important
feeling to foster on an earth that needs protecting.

It is interesting to wonder about the relationship be-
tween the Forts and the development of the children's
environmental action group named CAKE that was

born at this school. **Since the Forts predate the CAKE activities by twenty-five years, it is worth speculating about how much the connection with the earth through the Forts helped to bring the children to the awareness that enabled the styrofoam protest to take place.** *[author's emphasis]*

Maynard's final point is compelling. Authentic environmental commitment emerges out of firsthand experiences with real places on a small, manageable scale. These students' deep involvement in the Forts, with independence and autonomy ensured by the teachers, perhaps created the matrix, the fertile soil, in which true values of ownership and commitment could grow. Feeling like they owned the Forts, the children gained a sense of authority and empowerment. It was then an appropriate, accessible step to take on a local, visible issue like styrofoam.

When empathy and exploration are supported at the appropriate, critical periods in children's development, connectedness with the earth can serve as a wellspring for social action.

Bonding to the Self and Society

In most traditional cultures, rites of passage at puberty mark the end of childhood and the beginning of adulthood. These rites normally occur somewhere between ages eleven and fourteen. One of the primary functions of this ceremonial transition is to initiate the individual into social responsibility, into playing a role in the health and maintenance of the social order. The burgeoning energy of puberty, the child's new intellectual capacities, the ability to understand metaphor and complexity, are all channeled into new appropriate tasks that serve the community and give meaning to the individual's life.

Beginning at adolescence, students' alienation from society is an intractable problem facing American schools. Instead of bestowing new responsibilities on children, we keep them locked away in schools. We promise that we're preparing them for their future lives as adults, but real responsibility seems like a mirage on a distant horizon. What we need, beginning in middle schools, is an orientation toward service. Environmental projects that serve the community show students the relevance of the curriculum and give community organizations an injection of youthful energy. Examples of service initiatives conducted by middle school children (sixth and seventh graders seem to dominate) can serve as beacons for other children and teachers to follow.

An article in the March/April 1989 issue of *Sierra* relates how a group of sixth graders at Jackson Elementary School in Salt Lake City got concerned when they noticed that a map of hazardous waste sites in the city included a location just three blocks from their school. "'That old barrel yard?,' eleven-year-old Maxine asked, shocked at how close the site was to us. 'Kids climb all over those barrels.'" When classroom teacher Barbara Lewis contacted the Department of Health and was told that "there's nothing children can do. They'll be in high school before they see any results," the children were compelled to act. The students contacted the EPA, the owner of the barrel yard, and the mayor. They studied literature on hazardous waste and the problems involved in cleaning it up. They attracted reporters intrigued with the children's persistence at taking on such a knotty problem. And, after a year and a half, they not only witnessed removal of the 50,000 barrels and the beginnings of an EPA clean up, but they wrote legislation, lobbied legislators, and saw the passage of a Utah state law that set up a hazardous waste clean-up fund.

But social change projects don't have to be grandiloquent and adversarial to be successful. In Springfield, Vermont, a partnership program between the Riverside Middle School and the solid waste district is getting students into the community and solid waste managers into the school. After getting an overview of trash problems and how recycling can play a part in saving the town money and making it a safer place to live, groups of students are asked to devise projects that will contribute to the local effort. Kristin Forcier and Lauren Ellis, seventh graders in Pat Magrosky's class, conducted on-the-street surveys and found that only half of the people in the community recycled their household batteries. The rest of the batteries were either going into the landfill or getting incinerated, potentially causing groundwater or air pollution.

Lauren expressed her concern and emergent understanding when she said, "I didn't really think that throwing away a can of Raid was that bad until we did this project. When I was little, I didn't really think about it. I just thought my water comes from the faucet and it's clean and it's perfect. Unless, it comes from near the landfill. Then it's just like spraying a can of Raid in your mouth."

So Kristin and Lauren decided to make recycling batteries easier. They got permission from downtown stores to set up battery collection sites at the Price Chopper market, the Citgo station, the Ames department store, and the Bibens hardware store. They presented the idea to the Springfield Recycling Committee and received a commitment to have volunteers collect the batteries from the collection sites. And they created large informational signs and brochures for each of the collection sites that explain why battery recycling is important for the community. When asked what she had learned from the project, Lauren commented, "A kid can do it, with the help of adults."

Though I have portrayed each of these phases separately, they are not mutually exclusive. In real life there will always be a complex interplay of empathy, exploration, and social action. Empathy doesn't stop when exploration starts and social action does have a place in early childhood. Exploration of the natural world begins in early childhood, flourishes between ages seven and eleven, and should be sustained in adolescence as a pleasure and a source of strength for the demands of social action. Social action activities will be suitable during both of the previous phases when the scope is local and manageable.

For instance, after doing the weekly shopping with my seven-year-old daughter and four-year-old son one spring, we would put the groceries in the car and take a short walk across the meadow behind the shopping center to an unused railroad trestle. Our main focus was mastering their fear of walking on the deck of the bridge, looking through the railroad ties at the moving water below and seeing how far each of them could walk without holding my hand. I'd probably call it an exploration activity.

On the way to and fro, however, we'd also fill up plastic bags with discarded garbage from alongside the path. The kids named that activity "Cleaning up Mother Earth." It was a short walk. We probably only did five minutes of picking up, but week to week, it was easy to see the progress we were making. This kind of social action seems suitable and fitting for children of this age, especially when part of an engaging kinesthetic adventure. But the big challenge is to watch out for the downward creep of our activist inclinations, allowing children the un-adult-erated communion with nature that provides "intimations of immortality."

TAKING TIME: ALLOWING COMMUNION WITH NATURE

I WENT CANOEING with my six-year-old son, Eli, and his friend Julian this past April. The plan was to canoe a two-mile stretch of the Ashuelot River, an hour's paddle in adult time. Instead, we dawdled along for four or five hours. We netted golf balls off the bottom of the river that had been swept down from the upstream golf course. The boys were thrilled by this unplanned activity. We spent a lot of time looking down into the shallows and depths of the river with a purpose, and we wound up doing a lot of fish and bug watching too. We stopped at the mouth of a tributary stream for a picnic and went for a long adventure through a maze of marshy streams and abandoned floodplain oxbows. Following beaver trails led to "doing bridges"—balance-walking on fallen trees to get across marshy spots without getting our feet wet. We tiptoed across the tops of beaver dams, hopped hummocks, went wading (Eli called it "shallowing"), looked at spring flowers, tried to catch a snake, got lost and found. How fine it was to move at a meandery, child's pace.

The temptation to rush down the river is a trap waiting to catch parents and educators. Suffering from the timesickness of trying to do too much too quickly, we infect our children with our impatience. Most nature study or environmental education in American elementary schools lasts a matter of weeks, maybe a month. As a result, depth is sacrificed for breadth, and there's little opportunity for immersion in the landscape. Instead, we make children do workbooks in kindergarten, we let seven year olds watch Jurassic Park, and we bombard them with tragic anxiety. After the Oklahoma City bombing in 1995, a sixth-grade teacher asked his students what they thought of the TV coverage and one student spoke for many of them when she said, "It's not good to show so much on TV because kids see children all bloody and dead and it makes us scared about growing up in the world."

Some teachers are putting on the brakes. JoAnne Kruzshak, a first- and second-grade teacher in Thetford, Vermont, spent all of last year doing a project on a local beaver pond and marsh. These first and second graders visited the pond, about a quarter mile from the school, once a week through all kinds of weather. "In the beginning," Kruzshak recalls, "I thought we'd run out of things to do and study by Thanksgiving. By March I realized that there was no way we could follow up on all the neat opportunities by the end of the year."

The Harris Center for Conservation Education, located in the Monadnock highlands of southwestern New Hampshire, is one of the environmental education centers also taking the long view in designing its programs. Harris Center educators take a multifaceted developmental approach with teachers and students in their local public schools. From grades two through five, environmental educators lead classroom activities and nearby field trips six to eight times a month. Students also visit the Harris Center for nighttime owl walks, fort building, map and compass treasure hunts, wild animal programs, and for an adventure-oriented summer camp. In the middle-school grades, children survey vernal pools, design and maintain trails, and participate in simulated planning sessions about moose hunting and other local issues. In high school, students participate in an internationally acclaimed air-monitoring program and study other regional and nationally oriented topics. Because there's a clearly designed developmental strategy over the whole twelve years of schooling, environmental educators and school staff have time to let children bond with the natural world during the elementary years. The Harris Center's school program brochure entitled "Turning Science Inside Out" says:

> By the end of their journey with the Harris Center, students will have watched birds, searched for amphibians and insects, studied animal tracks, mushrooms and wild foods, surveyed wetlands, mapped local watersheds, learned the geological history of mountains in their area and tested the air and river quality. With one foot in snowshoe and the other in muck, we trek together learning the sweetness that comes with knowing the terrain.

If we want children to flourish, to become truly empowered, then let us allow them to love the earth before we ask them to save it. Perhaps this is what Thoreau had in mind when he said, "The more slowly trees grow at first, the sounder they are at the core, and I think the same is true of human beings."

REFERENCES

Arbib, Robert. *The Lord's Woods*. New York: W. W. Norton and Co., 1971.

Chawla, Louise and Hart, Roger. "Roots of Environmental Concern," in *Paths to Co-existence*, D. Lawrence et. al., eds. Washington, DC: Environmental Design Research Association, 1988.

Chawla, Louise. "Children's Concern for the Natural Environment." *Children's Environments Quarterly*, 5.3, 1988.

Chawla, Louise. "Childhood Place Attachments," in *Place Attachment*, Altman, I. and Low, S., eds. New York: Plenum Press, 1992.

Dillard, Annie. *An American Childhood*. New York: Harper and Row, 1987.

Karr, Paul. "The Cake Crusade." Sanctuary: *The Journal of the Massachusetts Audubon Society*, April 1990.

Kellert, Stephen J. "Attitudes Towards Animals: Age-related Development Among Children." *Journal of Environmental Education*, 16.3, 1985.

Leach, C. "Rainforests or Our Forest: A Critique of Rainforest Study at the Early Elementary Level." Unpublished paper in the author's collection. Keene, NH: Antioch New England Graduate School, 1993.

Lewis, B. "The Children's Cleanup Crusade." *Sierra*, March/April 1989.

Louv, Richard. *Childhood's Future*. Boston: Houghton Mifflin, 1990.

Maslin, Janet. "Children's Books/Environment." *The New York Times Book Review*, August 30, 1992.

Maynard, Patrice O. "The Forts at the George C. Soule School." Unpublished paper in the author's collection. Keene, NH: Antioch New England Graduate School, 1990.

Mitchell, Lucy S. *Young Geographers*. New York: Teacher's College Press, 1934.

Moore, Steve. "What's Important." Unpublished paper in the author's collection. Keene, NH: Antioch New England Graduate School, 1992.

Pearce, Joseph C. *Magical Child*. New York: Dutton, 1977.

Peterson, Brenda. "Animal Allies." *Orion*, Spring 1993.

Shepard, Paul. *The Arc of the Mind*. New York: Parabola Books, 1982.

Sobel, David. *Children's Special Places: Exploring the Role of Forts, Dens and Bushhouses in Middle Childhood*. Tucson, AZ: Zephyr Press, 1993.

Stafford, Kim. *Having Everything Right: Essays of Place*. Lewiston, ID: Confluence Press, 1986.

BOOKS FOR CHILDREN

Empathy (Ages 4-7)

All the Places to Love, by Patricia McLachlan, paintings by Mike Wimmer. New York: HarperCollins, 1994.

Archie, Follow Me, by Lynne Cherry. New York: E. P. Dutton, 1990.

The Butterfly Boy, by Laurence Yep, pictures by Jeanne M. Lee. New York: Farrar, Straus and Giroux, 1993.

Chipmunk Song, by Joanne Ryder, illustrated by Lynne Cherry. New York: E. P. Dutton, 1987.

A Fairy Went A-Marketing, by Rose Fyleman, illustrated by Jamichael Henterly. New York: E.P. Dutton, 1987.

The Fox Went Out on a Chilly Night, by Peter Spier. New York: Doubleday, 1989.

Grandfather Twilight, by Barbara Berger. New York: Philomel, 1986.

I Would Tuck You In, by Sarah Asper-Smith, illustrated by Mitchell Watley. Seattle: Sasquatch Press, 2012.

Jangles: A Big Fish Story, by David Shannon. New York: Scholastic, 2012.

The Mousehole Cat, by Antonia Barber, illustrated by Nicola Bayley. New York: Macmillan, 1990.

My Father Doesn't Know About the Woods and Me, by Dennis Haseley. New York: Atheneum, 1988.

Rabbit Island, by Jorg Steiner. New York: Harcourt Brace Jovanovich, 1978.

The Salamander Room, by Anne Mazer, illustrated by Steve Johnson. New York: Alfred A. Knopf, 1991.

The Snail and the Whale, by Julia Donaldson, illustrated by Axel Scheffler. Mascot, NSW, Australia: Koala Books, 2006.

The Star Maiden, retold by Barbara Juster Esbensen, illustrated by Helen K. Davie. Boston: Little, Brown and Co., 1988.

Stellaluna, by Janell Cannon. New York: Harcourt, Brace and Co., 1993.

Waddles, by David MacPhail. New York: Abrams Books, 2011.

When I'm Sleepy, by Jane Howard, illustrated by Lynne Cherry. New York: E. P. Dutton, 1985.

Winnie the Pooh, by A. A. Milne. New York: Dutton, 1971.

Exploration (Ages 8-11)

Bear's Adventure, by Benedict Blathwayt. New York: Alfred A. Knopf, 1988.

The Church Mouse, by Graham Oakley. New York: Atheneum, 1972. (Also see *The Church Mice Spread Their Wings* and other church mouse books by the same author.)

A Couple of Boys Have the Best Week Ever, by Marla Frazee. New York: Harcourt, 2009

Flotsam, by David Wiesner. New York: Houghton Miflin, 2006.

Groundhog Weather School, by Joan Holub, illustrated by Kristin Sorra. New York: Putnam Juvenile, 2009.

The Jungle of Peril, by Patrick Burston, illustrated by Alastair Graham. Cambridge, MA: Candlewick Press, 1996.

Magic School Bus: Lost in the Snow, by Joanna Cole, illustrated by Carolyn Bracken. New York: Scholastic, 2003.

The Mapmaker's Daughter, by Mary-Claire Helldorfer, illustrated by Jonathan Hunt. New York: Bradbury Press, 1991.

My Father's Dragon, by Ruth Stiles Gannett. New York: Random House, 1948. (also see *Elmer and the Dragon* and *The Dragons of Blueland* by the same author)

Paddle-to-the-Sea, by Holling C. Holling. Boston: Houghton Mifflin, 1941.

Secret Water, by Arthur Ransome. Boston: David R. Godine, 1995.
Swift, by Robert Blake. New York: Philomel/Penguin, 2007.

Three Days on a River in a Red Canoe, by Vera B. Williams.
New York: Greenwillow Books, 1981.

To Climb a Waterfall, by Jean Craighead George, illustrated by
Thomas Locker, Philomel, 1995.

Warm As Wool, by Scott Russell Sanders, illustrated by Helen
Cogancherry. New York: Bradbury Press: 1992.

The Water's Journey, by Eleonore Schmid. New York: North-
South Books, 1989.

Where the River Begins, by Thomas Locker. New York: Dial
Books, 1984.

The Wind in the Willows, by Kenneth Grahame. New York:
Charles Scribner's Sons, 1981.

Social Action (Ages 12-14)

Andrew Henry's Meadow, by Doris Burn. New York: Coward-
McCann, 1965.

California Blue, by David Klass. New York: Scholastic, 1994.

Come Back, Salmon, by Molly Cone, photographs by Sidnee
Wheelwright. San Francisco: Sierra Club Books for Children,
1992.

The Evolution of Calpurnia Tate, by Jacqueline Kelly. New York: Henry Holt, 2009.

The Garden in the City, by Gerda Muller. New York: Dutton Children's Books, 1992.

Gwinna, by Barbara Berger. New York: Philomel, 1990.

Hoot, by Carl Hiassen. New York: Random House, 2002.

Julie of the Wolves, by Jean Craighead George. New York: Harper and Row, 1972.

The Lost Seal, by Diana McKnight and Dorothy Emerling. Lanham, Maryland: Rowan and Littlefield, 2006.

The Man Who Planted Trees, by Jean Giono, wood engravings by Michael McCurdy. Chelsea, VT: Chelsea Green, 1985.

The Maze, by Will Hobbs. New York: Avon Books, 1998.

Miss Rumphius, by Barbara Cooney. New York: Viking, 1982.

My Place, by Nadia Wheatley and Donna Rawlins. Brooklyn, NY: Kane/Miller, 1992

My Side of the Mountain, by Jean Craighead George. New York: Dutton, 1988.

The People Who Hugged the Trees, adapted by Deborah Lee Rose, illustrations by Birgitta Säflund. Niwot, CO: Roberts Rinehart, 1990.

Prince William, by Gloria Rand, illustrated by Ted Rand. New York: Henry Holt and Co., 1992.

A River Ran Wild, by Lynne Cherry. New York: Harcourt Brace and Co., 1992.

About the Author

David T. Sobel is a senior faculty member in the education department at Antioch University New England in Keene, New Hampshire. He consults and speaks widely on child development and place-based education for schools, environmental organizations, and the National Park Service. He has authored seven books and more than sixty articles on children and nature for educators, parents, environmentalists, and school administrators, and his most recent books are *Wild Play: Parenting Adventures in the Great Outdoors* and *Place- and Community-Based Education in Schools.* He was recognized as one of the Daring Dozen educational leaders in the United States in 2007 by *Edutopia* magazine. David works and plays in the Monadnock region of southwestern New Hampshire and is committed to cold-water swimming, the exploration of landscape nooks and crannies, and to joyfully embracing the gift of life on earth.

ABOUT ORION MAGAZINE

SINCE 1982, *Orion* has been a meeting place for people who seek a conversation about nature and culture that is rooted in beauty, imagination, and hope. Through the written word, the visual arts, and the ideas of our culture's most imaginative thinkers, *Orion* seeks to craft a vision for a better future for both people and planet.

Reader-supported and totally advertising-free, *Orion* blends scientific thinking with the arts, and the intellectual with the emotional. *Orion* has a long history of publishing the work of established writers from Wendell Berry, Terry Tempest Williams, and Barry Lopez to Rebecca Solnit, Luis Alberto Urrea, and Sandra Steingraber.

Orion is also grounded in the visual arts, publishing picture essays and art portfolios that challenge the traditional definition of "environment" and invite readers to think deeply about their place in the natural world. *Orion*'s website, www.orionmagazine.org, features multimedia web extras including slide shows and author interviews, as well as opportunities for readers to discuss *Orion* articles.

Orion is published bimonthly by The Orion Society, a nonprofit 501(c)3 organization, and is available in both print and digital editions.

Subscribe

Orion publishes six beautiful, inspiring issues per year. To get a free trial issue, purchase a subscription, or order a gift subscription, please visit www.orionmagazine.org/subscribe or call 888/254-3713.

Support

Orion depends entirely on the generous support of readers and foundations to publish the magazine and books like this one. To support *Orion*, please visit www.orionmagazine.org/donate, or send a contribution directly to *Orion* at 187 Main Street, Great Barrington, MA, 01230.

To discuss making a gift of stock or securities, or for information about how to include *Orion* in your estate plans, please call us at 888/254-3713, or send an e-mail to development@orionmagazine.org.

Shop

Head to the *Orion* website, www.orionmagazine.org, to purchase *Orion* books, organic cotton t-shirts, and other merchandise featuring the distinctive *Orion* logo. Back issues from the past thirty years are also available.

MORE BOOKS FROM ORION

ORION READERS

Orion Readers collect landmark *Orion* essays into short thematic volumes:

Change Everything Now. A selection of essays about ecological urgency.

Thirty-Year Plan: Thirty Writers on What We Need to Build a Better Future. An eloquent statement on the future of humanity.

Wonder and Other Survival Skills. A collection of thoughtful and inspirational writing on our relationship to the natural world.

Beyond Ecophobia: Reclaiming the Heart in Nature Education, by David Sobel. An expanded version of one of *Orion's* most popular articles that speaks to those interested in nurturing in children the ability to understand and care deeply for nature from an early age.

Into the Field: A Guide to Locally Focused Learning, by Claire Walker Leslie, John Tallmadge, and Tom Wessels, with an introduction by Ann Zwinger. Curriculum ideas for teachers interested in taking their students out of doors.

Place-Based Education: Connecting Classrooms & Communities, by David Sobel. A guide for using the local community and environment as the starting place for curriculum learning, strengthening community bonds, appreciation for the natural world, and a commitment to citizen engagement.

ORION ANTHOLOGIES

Finding Home: Writing on Nature and Culture from Orion *Magazine*, edited by Peter Sauer. An anthology of the best writing from *Orion* published from 1982 to 1992.

The Future of Nature: Writing on a Human Ecology from Orion *Magazine*, selected and introduced by Barry Lopez. An anthology of the best writing from *Orion* published from 1992 to 2007.

FOR EDUCATORS

Ideal for reading groups and academic course adoption, many *Orion* books are accompanied by a downloadable teacher's guide consisting of key discussion questions. Teacher's guides can be found on the *Orion* website at www.orionmagazine .org/education.

Series design by Hans Teensma,
principal of the design studio Impress
(www.impressinc.com), which has
designed *Orion* since 1998.
The typeface is Scala, designed by Dutch
typographer Martin Majoor in 1990.
Printed by BookMobile.